The Chicago Bulls

The BEST Ever

By David Levine

A Sports Illustrated For Kids Book

The Chicago Bulls: The Best Ever
A SPORTS ILLUSTRATED FOR KIDS Book/January 1997

Cover and interior design by Beth P. Bugler

For information, address: SPORTS ILLUSTRATED FOR KIDS

The Chicago Bulls is published by SPORTS ILLUSTRATED FOR KIDS, a division of Time Inc. Its trademark is registered in the U.S. Patent and Trademark Office and in other countries. SPORTS ILLUSTRATED FOR KIDS, 1271 Avenue of the Americas, New York, NY 10020

PRINTED IN THE UNITED STATES OF AMERICA
10 9 8 7 6 5 4 3 2 1

ISBN 1-886749-23-X

Front cover photo: John McDonough/Sports Illustrated
Back cover photos: Andrew D. Bernstein/NBA Photos (Dennis Rodman), Manny Millan/Sports Illustrated (inset).

The Chicago Bulls is a production of SPORTS ILLUSTRATED FOR KIDS Books: Cathrine Wolf, Editorial Director; Margaret Sieck, Senior Editor; Jill Safro, Stephen Thomas (Project Editor), Associate Editors, Sherie Holder, Assistant Editor

Table of Contents

This book is dedicated to three special kids: Maggie, Carolyn, and Michael Levine

Introduction

On the Edge

The Chicago Bulls were in trouble. For only the second time in the entire 1995–96 season, they had lost two games in a row. And what a time to do it! In the NBA Finals! The Bulls had won the first three games of the series, beating the Seattle SuperSonics by a combined 43 points. The Sonics had come back and won two straight games. Now, they appeared to be in control of the series. What was going on? This wasn't the way the season was supposed to end!

The 1995–96 season had been like a dream come true for the Bulls. Michael Jordan was back for his first full season after an 18-month retirement. With Michael leading the way and supported by great players such as Scottie Pippen, Dennis Rodman, and Toni Kukoc *[COO-coach]*, Chicago had soared to an amazing 72–10 record in the regular season. That was an all-time NBA record for most wins in a season. The Bulls' season had been historic!

But as Michael, Scottie, and the rest of the Bulls would tell anyone who asked, "72–10 don't mean a thing without the ring." In other words, it's great to make history, but it's a whole lot more important to win an NBA title.

Without that championship, history doesn't mean much.

After the first few rounds of the playoffs, it looked as though Chicago's dream would end sweetly. They steamrolled the Miami Heat, the New York Knicks, and the Orlando Magic in the first three rounds. Against those three teams, the Bulls won 11 games and lost only one! Then came the Sonics.

Chicago led the series, 3–0. One win. That was all they needed to win their fourth title in six seasons. Most people thought the Bulls would have no trouble, that they would beat the SuperSonics in Game 4 of the Finals and complete the sweep. When they did, they would prove that the 1995–96 Bulls were one of the best teams in the history of the NBA. But then, something funny happened. Led by forward Shawn Kemp and point guard Gary Payton, the Sonics stomped Chicago, 107–86, in Game 4. Then, in Game 5, the Sonics beat the Bulls, 89–78.

BETTER THAN THE BULLS?

Before the 1995–96 Chicago Bulls won 72 games, the best regular-season record in NBA history belonged to the 1971–72 Los Angeles Lakers. Led by all-time greats Wilt Chamberlain and Elgin Baylor, the Lakers finished the season with a record of 69–13. Between November 5, 1971, and January 7, 1972, the Lakers won a league-best 33 games in a row, which is still an NBA record. During the 1995–96 season, the Bulls never won more than 18 in a row.

The Bulls had not been in this position all year long. They had always been the team in control. They had lost two games in a row only once all year — and that had happened more than four months earlier! Could they turn things around?

That is the test of a great team: how it responds when things are not going well. Great teams don't panic when things don't work out as planned. Great teams play better. Great teams rise to the occasion. All season long, people had been saying the Bulls were a great team. Now they had to prove it.

They did. In Game 6, the Bulls raced to a 6-point lead in the first quarter and they never trailed. Michael scored 22 points and Dennis Rodman had 19 rebounds as the Bulls won, 87–75. The NBA championship was theirs!

After the game, Michael lay on the floor in the trainer's room in the Bull locker room and cried. "It was hard," he said. "But winning a championship is supposed to be hard. I think this is the way it was meant to be."

Chicago had won 72 games in the regular season and 15 playoff games. That's 87 wins in one season. The Bulls lost only 13 games. They won their fourth NBA championship in six seasons. The 1995–96 Chicago Bulls were the best basketball team of all time.

Chapter One

The Early Years

Chicago, Illinois, is a great sports city. It has two baseball teams (the Cubs and the White Sox), a hockey team (the Blackhawks), and a football team (the Bears). Each of those teams has won a championship in its sport. But not one of them comes *close* to matching the success of the Bulls.

The Bulls have dominated professional basketball in the 1990's. Chicago has won four titles in six seasons. But until then, Chicago's basketball history hadn't always been so sweet.

The Chicago Bulls were created in 1966, when the National Basketball Association (NBA) added one team to the nine-team league. A group of businessmen led by former pro basketball player Dick Klein paid $1.6 million for the right to start a team in Chicago. The night before the new team's first press conference, Mr. Klein still needed a name for his team. "All I could think of was *Bulls*," he said.

Mr. Klein could have called them the *Nobodies*, because nobody in Chicago cared about them! The team only sold about 100 season tickets for their home games at Chicago Stadium. For the entire season, the Bulls drew an average of only 4,772 fans per game. Chicago Stadium seated more than 17,000 people, so there were a lot of empty seats!

The people of Chicago might not have cared, but the Bulls actually played well in their first season. They won 33 games. That is still a record for wins by an expansion (new) team. But the biggest surprise of all was that the Bulls made the playoffs! They lost in the first round. But just making the playoffs was a great thing for a new team.

Chicago's best player that first season was Jerry Sloan. Jerry was a 6' 6" guard. He was in his second NBA season. He was Chicago's first superstar. In 10 seasons with the Bulls, Jerry averaged 14.7 points and 7.7 rebounds per game.

As good as Jerry was, he couldn't carry the Bulls by himself. In their second season, the Bulls won 29 games and attendance fell to fewer than 4,000 per game. Very often, there were fewer than 1,000 people in the stands. Once,

ALL YOU NEED IS LOVE: BOB LOVE

Until Michael came along and broke his record, the Bulls' all-time leading scorer was a sweet-shooting guard named Bob Love. By the time he left the Bulls, in 1976, Bob had scored 12,623 points. Michael entered the 1996–97 season with 24,489 points in a little more than 10 seasons. That's almost twice as many as Bob!

In his eight-season career with the Bulls, Bob led the team in scoring seven times. He was also a three-time All-Star and was named to the NBA's all-defensive team three times. He retired in 1977, and the Bulls retired his jersey in 1994.

there were fewer than 600! When the Bulls announced that night's attendance, NBA commissioner Walter Kennedy got angry. He didn't want the world to know that things weren't going well with the young team. He yelled at the team for reporting such a low attendance figure — even though the figure was true!

Things began to look up by the early 1970's. From 1970 to 1975, the Bulls averaged 52 wins per season. In 1971, they had their first winning season. In 1974, they won their first playoff series. And in 1975, they made it all the way to the conference finals, just one series away from the championship round. The Bulls even led the Golden State Warriors in that series, 3 games to 2, before losing. Chicago wouldn't come that close to a title again for a *long* time.

In the eight seasons between 1976 and 1984, Chicago went through seven coaches. The Bulls were such big losers that they made the playoffs only once between 1977 and 1984! That's saying a lot, because even teams with losing records sometimes made the playoffs.

But in the wonderful world of pro sports, losing does have its reward: The teams with the worst records get first crack at the best new players. The Bulls finished the 1983–84 season with the third-worst record in the NBA, so they got the third pick in the 1984 draft of college players. With that pick, the Bulls selected a 6' 6" guard from the University of North Carolina.

His name was Michael Jordan.

Chapter Two

The Wait Is Over

Michael Jordan didn't suddenly appear out of thin air. People knew that he would be a good pro basketball player. He was, after all, the third player taken in the 1984 draft. But nobody knew that he would be very good. Remarkably good. *Scary* good.

The instant Michael put on a Chicago uniform, the Bulls became a better team. They qualified for the playoffs in each of his first six seasons. Michael made Chicago a *good* team all by himself. But he didn't make the Bulls a *great* team all by himself.

After he had been in the league a few years, fans began to say that Michael wasn't a really great player. Great players, such as Magic Johnson of the Los Angeles Lakers and Larry Bird of the Boston Celtics, make their teammates better. They won championships. Magic had helped the Lakers win five titles. Larry had led the Celtics to three titles. Michael hadn't led Chicago to any.

People started to call the Bulls "Michael and the Jordanaires." In other words, Chicago was like a musical group with a great lead singer (Michael) and four backup singers (the Jordanaires). To win a title, a team needs all five of its players working together.

The Bulls worked hard to change things. They acquired shooting guard John Paxson in 1985. In 1987, they drafted forward Horace Grant, and they got Scottie Pippen in a draft-day trade. Center Bill Cartwright came in a 1988 trade with the New York Knicks. The next year, they drafted guard B.J. Armstrong. Things haven't been the same since.

The Bulls cruised through the regular season in 1990–91. They finished the season with a team-record 61 wins. Of those 61 wins, the biggest came just before the All-Star Game. It was against the Detroit Pistons, the two-time defending NBA champions. The Pistons had beaten the Bulls in the playoffs three straight seasons. The two teams had played twice that season and each had won once.

At halftime, the Bulls led, 44–41. But in the second half, Detroit took control. With about six minutes left in the game,

WORKING CLASS HERO: HORACE GRANT

Michael Jordan and Scottie Pippen got all the glory, but Horace Grant did all the dirty work. While those two flew all over the court, Horace fought for rebounds and defended the other team's strongest player.

Horace, a 6' 10", 235-pound forward, was the 10th player taken in the 1987 draft. In seven seasons with the Bulls, he hit 53% of his shots and averaged 12.6 points and 8.6 rebounds per game. In 1994, he signed with the Orlando Magic. Horace's twin brother, Harvey, plays for the Washington Bullets.

NATHANIEL S. BUTLER/NBA PHOTOS

Power forward Horace Grant provided the muscle and grabbed the rebounds on the Bulls' first three title-winning teams.

they led, 83–79. It was the kind of Bull-Piston game that Detroit usually won. But in the last 2:13, Chicago outscored the Pistons, 10–4, and won the game, 95–93. The Bulls proved to themselves that they were as good as Detroit.

"As I look back," Coach Phil Jackson told *The Chicago Tribune* after the season, "that game had to be the one where we began to have confidence in what we could do."

In the first two rounds of the playoffs, Chicago rolled over the New York Knicks and the Philadelphia 76ers. Next up, the Pistons — again!

The Pistons and the Bulls had been fierce rivals for four seasons. The teams hated each other. The Detroit players were known as The Bad Boys because they played *very* rough. Coach Jackson told the Bulls to be tough, but not rough. Chicago played every bit as hard as Detroit. The series wasn't even close. The Bulls swept the Pistons, 4–0. The Pistons were so stunned by the loss that many of them got up off the bench and left the court before the last game had ended!

Chicago was past the Pistons. The Bulls would play the Los Angeles Lakers in the NBA Finals. The league's two best players, Michael and Magic Johnson, were going head-to-head. "It's what you live for, right?" Magic said.

After Game 1 of the NBA Finals, it didn't look like the Bulls were ready to win a title. Michael missed what would have been a game-winning shot and the Lakers won, 93–91. Michael had played well, scoring 36 points and dishing out 12 assists. But John Paxson, Horace Grant, and Bill Cartwright scored just 18 points — total. It looked like the same old Bulls: too much Michael, too little everyone else.

The Bulls roared back and won Game 2 by 21 points. They also won Game 3, which was a nail-biter. With 3.4 seconds left in regulation, Michael hit a 14-foot jump shot to send the game into overtime. In the extra period, Michael scored 6 points and the Bulls won, 104–96. In Game 4, the Bulls held the Lakers to only 82 points, and won, 97–82.

A funny thing happened in Game 5: Michael wasn't the star! In the fourth quarter, John Paxson took over. After L.A. had tied the score at 93 with 6:13 to play, John scored 10 points. Thanks to John, the Bulls won the game, 108–101, and their first NBA title!

"It took seven years, but we won," Michael said after the game. "This should get rid of the stigma that this is a one-man team." No one doubted that Michael was the greatest player in the game. Now that the Bulls had won the title, he had proved he could be a great teammate, too!

Chapter Three

Start All Over Again

As the 1991–92 season began, basketball fans wondered if the Bulls could win a second straight title. In the 20 years between 1971 and 1991, only two teams, the Detroit Pistons and the Los Angeles Lakers, had been able to repeat as NBA champions.

History wasn't the only thing working against Chicago. A new book called *The Jordan Rules* criticized Michael. It said that he received special treatment from coaches and that he treated teammates badly. Some of Michael's teammates thought he deserved the criticism, and that caused tension.

Could the Bulls ignore their problems and play like champions?

The Bulls didn't waste any time showing that they could. They won 17 of their first 20 games. Now people wondered if Chicago would set the record for most wins during the regular season. At the time, the record was 69 wins, set in 1971–72 by the Los Angeles Lakers. The Bulls came close. They finished 67–15. They weren't the all-time best — yet! — but they were easily the best that season.

Michael led the league in scoring for the sixth straight season. He averaged 30.1 points per game. But the real story was Scottie Pippen. In 1991–92, Scottie became a great player. He averaged 21 points, 7.7 rebounds, and 7 assists per game. Michael was still the best player in the league, but Scottie was a close second!

Michael and Scottie didn't win 67 games by themselves. Horace Grant became an excellent power forward. He averaged 14.2 points and 10 rebounds per game. Guard B.J. Armstrong averaged a career-high 9.9 points per game.

The regular season had been easy. But the playoffs are always a different story.

Chicago met the Miami Heat in the first round of the playoffs. The Bulls won, three games to none. Next came the New York Knicks.

Chicago had won 14 straight games against New York. But the Knicks stunned Chicago by winning Game 1. The Bulls recovered and won the next two, but New York fought back to win Game 4. The series was tied, 2–2. Through four games, the Knicks had held the Bulls to 88.8 points per game. That was more than 21 points below the Bulls' regular-season scoring average!

The Bulls hate playing the Knicks. Michael and Scottie are great at creating scoring opportunities on the fly. Teams like the Knicks try to slow down Michael and Scottie by grabbing them and fouling them almost every time they drive to the basket. "Their methods are no different from what Detroit's used to be," Michael said after Game 4. Coach Jackson was so angry at the way the Knicks played that he was thrown out of one game for arguing with a referee.

THE SHOTS HEARD 'ROUND CHICAGO

Of all the great shots Michael has hit in his career, these two *really* stand out:

• Game 5, first round of the 1989 playoffs: The Bulls lost all six of their regular-season games against the Cleveland Cavaliers. The Cavs led Game 5, 100–99 with three seconds left. If the Bulls lost, their season was over. Michael hit an 18-foot jumper with Cleveland's Craig Ehlo in his face. The Bulls won, 101–100.

• Game 4, 1993 Eastern Conference semi-finals: The Bulls led the Cavs, three games to none. But in Game 4, the score was tied at 101. The Bulls had the ball and one last chance. Just as he had four years earlier, Michael made a buzzer-beater to send the Cavs home. The Bulls, however, went on to win their third straight title.

Luckily for the Bulls, the series returned to Chicago. The Bulls won Game 5, 96–88. But in Game 6, Michael hit just nine of 25 shots, and the Knicks won, 100–86. Then, in Game 7, the greatest player in the NBA put on a great performance. Michael scored 42 points, and the Bulls destroyed the Knicks, 110–81. "This series was like a slap in the face," Michael said after the win.

In the conference finals, Chicago faced the Cleveland Cavaliers. After four games, the series was tied. Early in the series, Michael and Scottie played badly. But in Games 5 and 6, they began to hit their shots. The Bulls won the series, 4–2. Now Chicago would have a chance to defend its title.

This time, the Bulls' opponent in the Finals were the Portland Trail Blazers. Before the series, reporters asked

Michael to compare his game to the game of Portland's Clyde Drexler. Many people thought that Clyde was the second-best player in the league. Michael said that Clyde was a better 3-point shooter than he was. But Michael also said that he had never really *tried* to be a 3-point shooter.

In Game 1, Michael tried — and he went wild! In the first half, he hit six 3-pointers. By halftime, he had scored 35 points, and the Bulls led by 15. The game was over.

But these Bulls just couldn't do anything easily: They lost two of the next three games. They won Game 5 by 13 points, then struggled again in Game 6. Entering the fourth quarter of Game 6, Scottie had managed to hit just four of his 12 shots, and Michael was exhausted. No surprise then, that the Blazers led by 15.

Coach Jackson decided to try something different to start the last quarter. Chicago opened the quarter with a lineup that included Scottie and four subs (players who don't start). While Michael sat on the bench, the Bulls managed to erase the Blazer lead. Chicago outscored Portland 33–14 in the final quarter. The Bulls won, 97–93.

After the game, a reporter asked Michael if he had thought the Bulls could come back and win. "In my mind, frankly, no," he said. "I didn't think it was possible." It had been nearly impossible, but the Bulls had done it. Champs again!

Chapter Four

ThreePeat? ThreePeat!

In the history of the NBA, only two NBA teams had ever won three straight titles. They were the Minneapolis Lakers, from 1952 to 1954, and the Boston Celtics, who won an amazing eight straight between 1959 and 1966.

The Bulls knew it wouldn't be easy to become the third. Michael and Scottie had played for the Dream Team in the 1992 Summer Olympics. Would they be tired? John Paxson and Bill Cartwright had both had knee surgery. B.J. Armstrong replaced John as the point guard. Michael didn't think this was a good move. Players were critical of one another and complained publicly. All in all, things didn't look good.

The Bulls didn't play like the Bulls in 1992–93. But a bad Bull team is still better than most teams. By the end of the season, they were fighting for the best record in the Eastern Conference. Then the Bulls lost their last two games. The New York Knicks won the conference by three games.

As usual, Michael won the scoring title, his seventh straight, but he didn't win the MVP award. Like Michael, the Bulls had been good all year, but they hadn't been great.

Luckily, the first two playoff rounds were easy. Chicago

swept the Atlanta Hawks, 3–0, and the Cleveland Cavaliers, 4–0. For a team that had been struggling, 7–0 looked good. Next, they would play the Knicks.

The Bulls relied on John Paxson's solid ball handling and his accurate outside shooting.

The series opened in New York's Madison Square Garden. With the Knicks' wild and crazy fans shouting themselves silly, New York shut down the Bulls in Game 1. Michael made only 10 of 27 shots, and the Bulls lost, 98–90. Game 2 was no better, and Michael was even worse. He made only 12 of 32 shots as New York won again, 96–91. A few years earlier, the Bulls had been the young team anxious to beat the champs. The Knicks thought it was their turn.

NATHANIEL S. BUTLER/NBA PHOTOS

Too bad. Back in Chicago for Game 3, the Bulls walloped the Knicks, 103–83. Michael almost won Game 4 by himself. He scored 54 points and led Chicago to a 105–95 win. Michael had found his game, and Chicago was in control. In Game 5, he scored 29

A REAL STRAIGHT SHOOTER: JOHN PAXSON

John Paxson wasn't a flashy player, but that didn't matter. As the Bull point guard, he was responsible for running the team's offense. And John ran the offense very well. Coach Phil Jackson trusted him, and Michael Jordan *loved* playing with him.

What made John great was what he didn't do: He almost never made mistakes. He was also a *very* accurate shooter. In his best season, 1986–87, John averaged 11.3 points per game. By the time he retired, in 1994, John had played 11 seasons, nine with the Bulls. John's dad and his brother, both named Jim, played in the NBA.

points and had 14 assists. The Bulls won, 97–94, and took a 3–2 lead in the series.

Chicago won Game 6, 96–88, because Scottie Pippen took charge late in the game. In the final five minutes, he hit three huge baskets, each of which dropped through the hoop just before the 24-second clock expired. The Phoenix Suns were all that stood between Chicago and history.

At first, the Finals were no contest. Michael was a man on a mission. He scored 31 points in Game 1 and 42 in Game 2, and Chicago won both.

The Suns turned things around in Game 3. It took three overtimes and a little luck, but they pulled it out. With 6:20 left to play in regulation, the Suns led by 11, but Chicago roared back to force overtime. In the second overtime, the Bulls led by four with 40 seconds left. Somehow, the tired Suns won, 129–121.

The Bulls came right back and won Game 4, 111–105. Michael scored 55 points. Chicago led the series 3–1. The threepeat was just one game away. But, once again, the Suns rallied. They won Game 5, 108–98.

Game 6 started well for Chicago. Scottie and B.J. combined to score 42 points through three quarters, and the Bulls led by 8 points. But in the first 6:09 of the fourth quarter, they missed nine shots and turned the ball over twice. Phoenix scored 7 straight points. With 1:30 left in the game, the Suns led, 98–94.

The Bulls refused to lose. Michael's basket with 38.1 seconds left cut the lead to 98–96. But on the next possession, the Suns' Dan Majerle *[MAR-lee]* fired an airball! Chicago's ball! There were 14.1 seconds left.

Everybody *knew* that Michael would get the ball. He did, but he was covered. So he passed to Scottie . . . who passed to Horace . . . who passed to John . . . who was all alone near the 3-point line. John jumped into the air with 3.9 seconds left. He released the ball. It rose up and up, then fell softly through the net. Bulls 99, Suns 98. Bulls win! Bulls win! *Bulls win!*

After the game, Sun coach Paul Westphal talked about John's shot and the Chicago Bulls. "You play all year, and it comes down to this — every eye in the arena following the ball. It seemed as if it were in the air for an hour. Every kid dreams of that in his backyard, and Paxson got to live out his dream. It was a great shot. We lost to a great team."

One of the best.

Chapter Five

Back on Top

The Chicago Bulls were three-time champions. It seemed likely they could make it four in a row. Then, something happened that *nobody* had expected to happen. Michael Jordan retired.

Michael made his announcement just before the 1993–94 season. He said he had lost the desire to play. He was tired of traveling, and he was tired of the media. He was sad because his father, James, had been murdered just a few months earlier. He wanted to get away. He wanted to stay home and spend time with his family.

The Bulls were in a jam. No team can lose their best player — let alone the best player in *history* — without suffering. The Bulls suffered. Though they did make the playoffs in 1994 and 1995, they lost in the second round each time.

The Bulls made other changes after Michael left. In fact, most of the team was rebuilt. John Paxson retired. Bill Cartwright, B.J. Armstrong, and Horace Grant went to other teams. Only Scottie Pippen stayed.

Chicago picked up other good players. In 1990, the Bulls drafted Toni Kukoc, a superstar forward who played in Europe. Toni finally joined the team in 1993. Guard Steve Kerr joined the team the same year. Center Bill Wennington came aboard the following year. Later, center Luc Longley and guard Ron Harper were added.

But in the spring of 1995, the most important player rejoined the team: Michael. He decided he missed basketball. He returned to the Bulls in time to play 17 regular-season games and the playoffs. His real goal, though, was to win the NBA title in 1996.

Michael wasn't the only "new" Bull player in 1995–96. Chicago also added Dennis Rodman. Not everyone on the Bulls was thrilled to have Dennis as a teammate. He had played for the Detroit Pistons during the frustrating years before Chicago won its first title. Dennis had been one of the Detroit players whom the Bulls hated. Scottie Pippen *really* didn't want Dennis on the team. Scottie remembered the time that Dennis pushed him down on purpose. Scottie had been lucky that he wasn't seriously hurt.

But the Bulls knew that Dennis was the kind of player they needed. He was a powerful forward and a terrific rebounder. Chicago needed to rebound better. Bull fans expected great things. Boy, did they get great things!

In the 1995–96 season's first game, Michael scored 42 points, and the Bulls beat Charlotte. They won four more games before losing. Then, they won their next game. That was something they did all year: come back to win after a loss. Chicago lost two games in a row only once all season!

By the All-Star break, Chicago was 42–5. It was clear they would have the best record in basketball — by far. But could the Bulls set the record for most wins in a season? In 1991–92, they had missed tying the record (69 wins) by two victories. Would they win 70 this time?

After the All-Star break, people really began talking about 70 wins. Dennis tried not to listen. "It's a stupid goal," he said. "It gets you thinking about all the wrong things, and it means nothing if you don't win a championship."

Chicago's only rough spot came in March. Before he joined the Bulls, Dennis had become famous for his outrageous behavior. Once, he gave someone in the stands his shoes and sat on the bench in just his socks! But since coming to Chicago, he had stayed out of trouble — until a March 16 game against the New Jersey Nets. Dennis head-butted a referee and was suspended for six games. Without Dennis, the Bulls still won five out of six. When he returned, Chicago was 63–8. It was only a matter of time

JAMMING WITHOUT JORDAN

What do you do when the best player in basketball history retires from your team? Give up, right? *Wrong.* Even without Michael, the 1993–94 Bulls were one of the best teams in the NBA.

Led by Scottie Pippen, Horace Grant, and newcomer Toni Kukoc, the Bulls were 55–27 in the regular season. In the first round of the playoffs, they swept the Cleveland Cavaliers, 3–0. In the Eastern Conference semi-finals, they faced their rivals, the New York Knicks. Despite losing the first two games of the series, the Bulls fought back. In the end, the Knicks won a thrilling seven-game series.

before Chicago broke the record for wins in a regular season — and not much time at that.

On April 16, 1996, the Bulls did it. They beat the Milwaukee Bucks, 86–80, for their 70th victory. Before the season was over, Chicago pushed its record to 72–10. Even Michael was impressed. "This puts our names in the history books," he said. But setting the record "doesn't have the same effect as winning a championship," he said.

So Michael and the Bulls turned to that task.

Was there any doubt that the Bulls would win their fourth championship in six seasons? Not much.

The Bulls swept the Miami Heat in the first round of the playoffs, 3–0. Next, they beat the Knicks, 4–1. After that, it was good-bye Orlando Magic. The Bulls swept them, 4–0.

The Seattle SuperSonics, Chicago's opponent in the Finals, thought they had a chance to win. Seattle *was* good: While everyone was focused on the Bulls' run at the record, the Sonics had

SURE, THE BULLS ARE GOOD, BUT . . .

Most folks agree that Michael is the best player to put on an NBA uniform. But if he and the Bulls hope to catch the all-time champion of champions, they have their work cut out for them. Between 1957 and 1969, the Boston Celtics won 11 titles. Hall of Fame center Bill Russell was the star of every one of those teams. Bill has more championship rings than he does fingers!

BARRY GOSSAGE/NBA PHOTOS

Ron Harper and the Bulls soared back to the top in 1996.

quietly won 64 games of their own. Even so, the Bulls were still big favorites to win.

In Game 1 of the Finals, the Bulls played tough defense. They kept the high-scoring Sonics from "running and gunning." But after three quarters, the Bulls led just 79–77. In the fourth quarter, Toni Kukoc scored 10 straight points to help Chicago take control. The Bulls won, 107–90.

Dennis had scored 7 points and grabbed 16 rebounds in Game 1. But, he was even better in Game 2. Chicago also won that game, 92–88. Dennis pulled down 20 rebounds, which was not unusual. He also scored 10 points. "He was their MVP tonight," Seattle coach George Karl said of Dennis.

Chicago wasted no time trouncing the Sonics in Game 3. Michael scored 27 points in just the first half! The Bulls led 63–28 at halftime and won going away, 108–86. "That was a spectacular game," Coach Jackson said afterwards. "It was one of the best we've played all season and probably our best in the playoffs." They led the series three games to none. One more win would do it.

But remember, Seattle *did* win 64 games in the regular season. The Sonics *were* a great team — and they fought back hard. Shawn Kemp and Gary Payton got hot. In Game 5, Shawn scored 25 points and grabbed 11 rebounds. Gary had 21 points and 11 assists. The Sonics led by 21 points at halftime and went on to win by 21, 107–86. Game 5 wasn't much better for the Bulls. Michael made 11-of-22 shots, but the rest of the Bulls made just 18-of-55. Seattle won, 89–78. Suddenly, the series was 3–2 and the Bulls were in trouble.

But Game 6 was all Chicago. Scottie scored 17 points, and Dennis had 19 rebounds. In one stretch of the third quarter, the Bulls outscored the Sonics 7 to zero to extend their lead to 17 points. Seattle's confidence was ruined. The Bulls won, 87–75.

By winning the series, 4–2, the Bulls had completed the most remarkable season in NBA history. They had 72 regular season wins, a 15–3 playoff record, and their fourth world championship in six seasons. Nobody could deny that this Bulls club was the greatest team ever.

Chapter Six

Michael Jordan

No, Michael Jordan can't leap tall buildings in a single bound like Superman. But there isn't much he can't do on a basketball court. Michael is amazing, the greatest player who ever lived — by far. But, like Superman, he's human too.

Michael Jordan was born on February 17, 1963. He grew up in Wilmington, North Carolina, a small city not far from the Atlantic Ocean. His father, James, worked at an electric plant. His mother, Deloris, worked at a bank. Mr. and Mrs. Jordan had five children. Michael had two older brothers, one older sister, and one younger sister.

When Michael was a kid, he pitched and played outfield in baseball. He also played quarterback in football and guard in basketball. When he was in ninth grade, he became very serious about basketball, so his dad marked out a court in the Jordan's back yard. "We played neighborhood games for at least two hours every day," Michael said. "On Saturdays, we were out there all day."

Michael often challenged his older brother, Larry, at basketball. No matter how hard Michael tried, he couldn't beat him. "Larry used to beat me all the time and I'd get mad," Michael once said. "We'd fight all the time. He created determination in me." Michael owes Larry, because if he hadn't taught him to be determined, Michael might not have become Air Jordan.

Name: **Michael Jordan**
Birth Date: **February 17, 1963**
1st Season in NBA: **1984**
Height: **6' 6"**
Weight: **216 pounds**
Nickname: **Air Jordan**

When Michael was a sophomore in high school, he tried out for the basketball team. He thought playing basketball would make him more cool, which was important to him. You see, Michael thought he was kind of funny looking, and he was afraid he would never have a girlfriend or a wife. Michael even took cooking and sewing classes so that he could take care of himself in the future!

Michael's best friend made the basketball team. So did Larry. But Michael didn't! The coach said that Michael, who was 5' 11" at the time, wasn't tall enough. "I was devastated," Michael said later. "It's like you want to put your head underneath your pillow, and you don't want to go to school."

Michael wouldn't give up, though. He continued to work on his game. He scored almost 30 points per game as a member of the junior varsity team. Then, during the summer before his junior year, he grew four inches! That year, he made the varsity squad. Before his senior year, Michael attended a basketball camp with other great high school players from around the country. Michael was the MVP of the camp! Before long, schools with great basketball programs were offering him scholarships. No one from Michael's high school had ever gone on to play for a major college basketball team. "I wanted to be the first," he said.

In the fall of his senior year, Michael accepted a scholarship to the University of North Carolina (UNC). It was a surprising choice. When he was a kid, Michael had rooted for North Carolina State University. David Thompson, Michael's hero, had been a star there. Michael's mom was a big fan of UNC, but Michael *hated* the school. In fact, Mrs. Jordan once got mad at Michael because he rooted against UNC in the 1977 NCAA championship game.

But Michael was happy. UNC is in Chapel Hill, not far from Wilmington. He would be close to his family. He would be playing for one of the finest teams in the nation, the Tar Heels, and one of the best coaches in college basketball history, Dean Smith.

Coach Smith is a tough coach. He doesn't usually let freshman start for North Carolina. But Coach Smith could not ignore Michael's talent, so he made him a starter in his first year, 1982. Good move, Coach.

As a freshman, Michael averaged 13.5 points per game. He was named the Atlantic Coast Conference rookie of the year. People in the southeast began to realize just how talented Michael was. Soon, the whole *country* would know.

Michael and the Tar Heels played Georgetown University in the NCAA championship game. Late in the

Michael Jordan's College Statistics

Season	Games	Points Total	Points Average	Assists Average	Rebounds Average
1981–82	34	460	13.5	1.8	4.4
1982–83	36	721	20.0	1.6	5.5
1983–84	31	607	19.6	2.1	5.3
Totals	**101**	**1,788**	**17.7**	**1.8**	**5.0**

game, Georgetown led, 62–61. With just 18 seconds left, Michael got the ball in the corner. Surrounded by Georgetown players, Michael jumped into the air and released a 16-foot jumper that dropped perfectly through the net. The Tar Heels won the game, 63–62. North Carolina was Number 1, and Michael was officially a star.

In each of the next two years, Michael was named college player of the year. He *owned* college hoops. He decided it was time to turn pro. In the spring of 1984, Michael announced that he was leaving North Carolina to enter the NBA draft.

A few months before his first pro season, Michael played for the U.S. in the 1984 Summer Olympics. U.S. fans already knew what Michael could do. The Olympics gave him a chance to show the *world*. The U.S. romped to the gold medal, and Michael was dazzling. Bobby Knight, the U.S. coach, said that Michael was the best player he had ever seen.

Even with all his college and Olympic success, no one knew how good Michael was. Back then, Coach Smith's teams played a conservative style. He didn't

TONI THE TIGER

Toni wasn't a starter in 1995–96, but he won the NBA's Sixth Man of the Year Award.

ANDREW D. BERNSTEIN/NBA PHOTOS

A LEAN, MEAN BASKETBALL MACHINE

Scottie can do it all. In 1993–94, when Michael didn't play, Scottie led the Bulls in scoring, assists, and steals, and was second in rebounding. In 1995–96, he averaged 19.4 points and 5.9 assists per game.

COME FLY WITH ME

With Michael leading the way, the Bulls flew over the rest of the NBA in 1995–96. Michael didn't miss a beat after 18 months away from the game. He won his eighth scoring title.

THE MAN BEHIND THE MAGIC

Head coach Phil Jackson is one of only nine men to win NBA titles as a player and coach. Phil played for the New York Knicks when they won championships in 1970 and 1973.

L S. BUTLER/NBA PHOTOS

HE MAN IN HE MIDDLE

lls' fans have tten used to eing Michael with e championship phy. After all, the lls did win it four nes in six years!

SCOTT CUNNINGHAM/NBA PHOTOS

D. BERNSTEIN/NBA PHOTOS

READ IT AND WEEP

This fan's banner says it all. Who's going to argue?

THE BEST. EVER. ANYWHERE.

HEY, THAT'S MY BALL!

Dennis Rodman *(center, in red)* and Luc Longley *(right)* fight Knicks Patrick Ewing *(top)* and Charles Oakley for the ball. In 1995–96, Dennis led the NBA in rebounding for the fifth straight year.

like flashy plays like dunks or behind-the-back passes. Michael wasn't allowed to really show his stuff in college. *No one* imagined that Michael would be an NBA superstar.

The Chicago Bulls selected Michael with the third pick in the 1984 draft. Chicago's owners and coaches had no idea what they had. "They were real happy, but it wasn't like, 'Wow, this is it,' " said Tim Hallam, the Bulls' public relations director. "They thought we had picked a solid player who would turn out to be good for the team, but not the greatest player in the league."

Michael was a little nervous about going to the pros. "I had never even been to Chicago. I didn't know anything about the city, nothing," he said. "I didn't know anything about the team except that it was bad. I didn't know any of the players, any of the past players, nothing. I didn't know much about the NBA at all."

Michael may not have known much then. But he learned quickly!

Michael was an immediate hit in the pros. In only his third game, he scored 37 points. For the season, Michael averaged 28.2 points per game. Not bad for a rookie — or even a seasoned veteran! No wonder Michael was named Rookie of the Year.

Michael's second season, 1985–86, wasn't as much fun. In the third game of the year, Michael broke a bone in his foot. He missed 64 games but returned to the team in time to help Chicago qualify for the playoffs for the second straight year.

In the first round, the Bulls played the Boston Celtics. In Game 2, Michael scored 63 points! No one had ever scored more points in a playoff game! Larry Bird, the Celtics' great forward, was amazed. "If God was a basketball player, He'd be Michael Jordan," Larry said. Still, the Bulls lost the series, three games to none.

Michael exploded in 1986–87, his third season. He scored 50 points in the first game! He never looked back. Michael led the league in scoring, with 37.1 points per game, the fifth-highest average ever. Hall of Fame center Wilt Chamberlain had the other four top averages. Michael was the best non-Wilt scorer in history!

By the time Michael was 25 years old, he had been in the league four years. He had won two scoring titles and one MVP award. Many people thought he was already the best who ever played. "I've seen some incredible players," Jerry West, the executive vice president of the Los Angeles Lakers said. "The Lakers have had some incredible players — Kareem Abdul-Jabbar, Magic Johnson — and it's awful to say, but Michael Jordan is the best player I've ever seen."

Seasons came and went, and Michael continued to amaze people. But the Bulls didn't. They made the playoffs every season and they lost in the playoffs every season. The Bulls didn't win an NBA title until 1991, Michael's seventh season. Then they won in 1992 . . . and *another* in 1993!

Michael was on top of the basketball world. He had won three MVP awards, and seven straight scoring titles. He had been an All-Star eight times, and he had led the

Bulls to three straight championships. When it came to basketball, there wasn't anything he couldn't do or hadn't done. So he left the NBA.

Michael retired for a lot of reasons. He was tired of traveling, tired of constant attention. He was also tired of writers and reporters who poked their noses into his private life. Michael had been criticized for his behavior off the court. Some people wrote that he had a serious gambling problem. Michael said he didn't. He was tired of all the attention and criticism.

But was that enough to make the world's greatest basketball player walk away from the game he loved? No, there was more — *a lot* more. In July 1993, Michael's father was murdered. Michael was devastated.

Mr. Jordan had been more than just a father to Michael. He had been Michael's best friend. As a result of his

A SCORING MACHINE

Entering the 1996–97 regular season, Michael had won eight scoring titles, more than any other player in NBA history. Between 1986–87 and 1992–93, Michael won seven straight scoring titles. That tied him with Wilt Chamberlain for the most consecutive scoring titles. After his 18-month retirement, Michael came back and won the 1995–96 scoring title. His career scoring average of 32 points per game was also the highest average in NBA history. Wilt Chamberlain is the only other player whose career average is over 30.

dad's death, Michael decided that he wanted to spend more time with his wife, Juanita, and their three kids. At a press conference in October to announce his retirement, Michael said that he had lost the desire to play basketball.

If Michael's retirement surprised people, so did his next announcement: He wanted to become a professional baseball player! Michael hadn't played baseball since high school. But Jerry Reinsdorf, the owner of the Bulls, also owned the Chicago White Sox. Mr. Reinsdorf knew how much Michael loved baseball and how much he wanted to play, so he signed him to a minor league contract. Michael went to Alabama to play for the Birmingham Barons, one of Chicago's minor league teams.

Everyone was curious to see how Michael would do as a baseball player. Before his first game, more than 10,000 people lined up outside the stadium to see him play. The

MICHAEL JORDAN, THE MAJOR LEAGUER?!?

Most people thought Michael was crazy when he announced that he wanted to become a baseball player. But it made perfect sense to Michael.

Michael had always loved baseball. He once said that his favorite childhood memory was of a one-hitter he pitched when he was 12 years old. In 1975, Michael was even named Mr. Baseball for North Carolina's 12-year-olds.

There was another reason Michael decided to follow his dream: Two years before his father was killed, Mr. Jordan had told Michael that he still sometimes dreamed of seeing his son in the major leagues.

Barons usually drew about 4,000 fans to a game. Michael's first performance was a disappointment: He went 0-for-3 with two strikeouts.

The rest of the season wasn't much better. His batting average was only .202, and he hit only three homers in 436 at-bats. He struck out a lot — 114 times — and committed 11 errors in the outfield. But Michael wasn't frustrated. "What I've done is give inspiration to people," Michael said. "Don't give up before you even try. If you don't succeed, then at least you know by giving it an opportunity."

Michael stuck with it, and he improved. In the fall of 1994, he played in the Arizona fall league and hit .252. Still, he called himself the team's worst player. Michael realized he wouldn't make it as a major leaguer. And, he had to admit, he missed basketball.

Michael loved basketball too much to stay away. In March 1995, he issued a statement to the press. It had only two words on it: "I'm back." Michael rejoined the Bulls for the last 17 games of the 1994–95 season.

During Michael's retirement, the Bulls had retired his number, 23. That meant that he wouldn't be allowed to wear 23 again unless he and the Bulls received permission from the NBA. Instead, Michael decided to wear 45, the number his brother Larry wore when they were kids.

Although the Bulls won 13 of their last 17 games, Michael wasn't the same player he'd been when he left 18 months before. He hit only 41 percent of his shots, way below his career average of 51 percent. Even worse for

Michael and the Bulls, he committed some *terrible* turnovers in the playoffs.

Michael was playing so poorly that he decided he needed to change his luck. Before Game 2 of the second-round of the playoffs against the Orlando Magic, Michael decided to wear his old number. Since the Bulls hadn't received the NBA's permission to use the number, they had to pay $100,000 in fines. It didn't matter. The team wanted the old Michael Jordan back.

The Bulls didn't get the old Jordan back immediately, but they got him in 1995–96 — and then some!

During the off-season, Michael worked hard to get in shape. He showed up for training camp in the fall "in the best shape I've ever been in." He was also more focused. He couldn't wait to play a full season again. "It's been a while since I looked forward to a basketball season like this," he said. "I feel like a kid, all excited."

In 1995–96, Michael played in his ninth All-Star game, won his fourth NBA title, his fourth MVP award, his fourth NBA Finals MVP award, his eighth scoring title . . . oh, and the Bulls won 72 regular-season games, more than any team in NBA history.

Michael was excited. The Bulls and their fans were thrilled!

Chapter Seven

Scottie Pippen

Somehow, some way, Scottie Pippen became an NBA superstar. One thing's for sure: No one had expected him to become a superstar.

Scottie wasn't much of a player when he was young. When he was in high school, not one major college recruited him. If it hadn't been for his high school coach, Scottie might not have gone to college. But he did, and somehow, some way, he continued to improve — until, one day, he had become an NBA superstar.

Scottie Pippen was born on September 25, 1965. When he got older, he changed the spelling of his name from *Scotty* to *Scottie*. He did it, he says, so that "people would know that it is a given name, not a nickname."

Scottie's parents, Preston and Ethel, had 12 children. Scottie is the youngest. The Pippens lived in Hamburg, Arkansas, a tiny town that had only one traffic light. Scottie had a tough childhood. When he was in ninth grade, his dad suffered a stroke, which damaged Mr. Pippen's brain. Mr. Pippen had to retire from his job. Unfortunately, that wasn't the only bad thing to happen to the Pippens: Scottie's brother Ronnie had an accident in gym class and was paralyzed.

Like a lot of kids, Scottie dreamed of playing in the NBA. But when he was a senior in high school, he was only 6' 1" and weighed just 135 pounds. That's puny by NBA standards. "Being the size I was then, I didn't have any big plans for basketball," Scottie once said.

No college wanted him. So Scottie's coach called a friend, Don Dyer, who coached the University of Central Arkansas Bears. Coach Dyer agreed to take Scottie. But Scottie would have to be the team manager! He could practice with the team but wouldn't play. As manager, he had to wash uniforms, hand out towels, and sweep the floor — hardly a job for a future NBA all-star!

Still, Scottie was happy. At least he had a chance. Then he started to grow. By the end of his freshman year, he was 6' 3". Coach Dyer let him play a bit. At the end of the season, Scottie was given a basketball scholarship. Goodbye dirty towels!

Best of all, Scottie kept growing. In his sophomore year, he hit 6' 5". By his senior year, he was 6' 7" and the Bears' best player. In four years he had grown six inches! He also grew into stardom. In 1986–87, his senior year, Scottie averaged 23.6 points, 10 rebounds and 4.3 assists per game. Suddenly, some NBA scouts began to notice him.

Name: **Scottie Pippen**
Birth Date: **September 25, 1965**
1st Season in NBA: **1987**
Height: **6' 7"**
Weight: **228 pounds**
Nickname: **Pip**

But how good was he? It was hard for the scouts to tell.

Central Arkansas was a very small school that played in a small league. Scottie had never faced really tough competition. NBA scouts figured he would be drafted, but not very high.

Each year before the NBA draft, college players go to camps where they play against other top college players. The camps give NBA teams a chance to look at players and decide whom they want to draft. It was the first time Scottie had played against top players. He did great!

Scottie Pippen's College Statistics

		POINTS		ASSISTS	REBOUNDS
Season	Games	Total	Average	Average	Average
1983–84	20	85	4.3	0.7	3.0
1984–85	19	351	18.5	1.6	9.2
1985–86	29	574	19.8	3.5	9.2
1986–87	25	590	23.6	4.3	10.0
Totals	**93**	**1,600**	**17.2**	**2.7**	**8.1**

Jerry Krause, the Chicago Bulls' general manager, loved what he saw. "Scottie had the longest arms I'd ever seen," Mr. Krause said. "The kid was a long-armed goose." Scottie was only 6' 7", but Mr. Krause thought his long arms made him seem as if he was 6' 11"!

The Bulls weren't the only team impressed with Scottie. Suddenly, a lot of teams were interested in him. The Bulls were afraid some team would draft Scottie before they could. So Mr. Krause made a deal: The Seattle SuperSonics would take Scottie with the fifth pick. The Bulls would take

ANDY HAYT/NBA PHOTOS

Scottie hasn't allowed anyone or anything to stand between him and stardom.

Olden Polynice with the eighth pick. Then, the two teams would swap players.

Scottie may have been the fifth player taken in the draft, but there still were a lot of people who didn't know who he was. "I never even heard of Scottie Pippen until two weeks ago," Reggie Williams said after the draft. Reggie was the *fourth* player taken!

It didn't take long for the rest of the NBA to hear about Scottie. And what they heard was that the kid could flat-out play! In each of his first five seasons in the league,

Scottie improved both his scoring and rebounding averages. He played in two All-Star games and for the U.S. Dream Team at the 1992 Summer Olympics.

There isn't much that Scottie doesn't do well. If he isn't scoring 20 points, he's grabbing eight or nine rebounds. If he isn't doing one of those two things, then he's dishing out four or five assists. Sometimes, he does all those things in the same game! "You look at him . . . his tools [skills] just stun you," said Mr. Krause.

Even so, after four seasons in the league, some people still wondered if Scottie had what it took to be a superstar. They thought that Scottie was soft. They pointed to two incidents that they believed proved their point.

In Game 6 of the 1989 Eastern Conference finals, Detroit Piston center Bill Laimbeer elbowed Scottie in the head. Scottie was knocked unconscious and didn't return to the game. The Bulls lost, 103–94, and were eliminated from the playoffs. The fans thought Scottie should have played. What they didn't know was that Scottie had *begged* the doctor to let him play.

One year later, the Bulls again faced the Pistons in the Eastern Conference finals. This time, in Game 7, Scottie missed most of the game with a serious headache. Once again, the Bulls lost and were eliminated from the playoffs. And, once again, people thought Scottie was being wimpy.

Scottie's reputation went downhill fast. There was only one way for him to change people's minds. He had to play great in big games. And the only games that really mattered were playoff games.

Scottie had plenty of chances to prove that he was tough because Chicago made the playoffs year after year. In 1991, the Bulls and the Detroit Pistons met in the playoffs for the fourth straight year. This time, Scottie ignored Detroit's rough tactics and helped Chicago sweep Detroit in four games. The Bulls went on to win their first NBA championship. In the 1992 and 1993 playoffs, Chicago played the New York Knicks. The Knicks bumped and fouled Scottie almost every time he touched the ball. But in both series, Scottie didn't pay any attention to his opponents' dirty tricks. He just played, and played well. Chicago won both series and two more championships.

Scottie buried his reputation as a wimp once and for all during Michael Jordan's 18-month retirement. Without Michael, it was up to Scottie to step up and carry the Bulls. That's exactly what he did. During the 1993–94 season, he led the Bulls in scoring (22.0 points per game), and assists (5.6), and was second in rebounding (8.7). The Bulls finished the season 55–27, the third-best record in the Eastern Conference. In 1994–95, he led the team in scoring (21.4), rebounding (8.1), and assists (5.2).

"You think about where he started, this quiet kid from Arkansas whom nobody had ever heard of,"said his agent, Jimmy Sexton. "It's amazing how far he's come."

When Michael was away, Scottie proved that he was a team leader and one of the top players in the league. When Michael returned to the lineup, the Bulls realized that they didn't have one, they had *two* NBA superstars in their lineup!

Chapter Eight

Dennis Rodman

Dennis Rodman is a wild man. He has so many tattoos he looks like a billboard. His hair seems to change color once or twice every week. He paints his fingernails. He has been known to dress up in women's clothes. And you don't even want to know how many different parts of Dennis's body have been pierced.

Dennis is an outrageous person. But he's also an outrageous rebounder. And that's what makes him and the Chicago Bulls an outrageous combination!

Dennis Rodman was born May 13, 1961. He grew up in a poor section of Dallas, Texas. Dennis lived with his mother and two sisters. His father left the family when Dennis was very young. "I felt shut out not having a father, always having to look out for myself," Dennis said.

Dennis wasn't very athletic when he was young. Mostly, he hung out with friends. Dennis didn't even play basketball in high school. At first, he didn't even go to college. After graduating from high school, Dennis spent three years doing odd jobs. He worked as a busboy cleaning tables in a restaurant. He worked as a janitor. He cleaned cars at an auto dealership. He also got into trouble.

When he was 19 years old, he was arrested for stealing. He spent a night in jail. "In that cell, I swore I was going to make something of myself," he said later.

When he was a senior in high school, Dennis was just 5' 11" tall. One year later, he was 6' 7". In 1982, he did well in a basketball tryout and was given a scholarship to Cooke County Junior College, a two-year school. If Dennis had done well, he might have been offered a scholarship to a Division I school. But he flunked out after one semester.

Name: **Dennis Rodman**
Birth Date: **May 13, 1961**
1st Season in NBA: **1986**
Height: **6' 8"**
Weight: **210 pounds**
Nickname: **The Worm**

Dennis went home to Dallas. He started hanging out again. He was 22 years old. So far, he hadn't done much with his life. "I figured I had to try again to get off those streets," he said.

A few months later, he was given another chance. Southeastern Oklahoma State University offered him a scholarship. A coach from the school had seen Dennis play at Cooke. He convinced Southeastern Oklahoma to give Dennis a chance.

Dennis committed himself to basketball. His friends thought he was crazy. He wasn't good enough, they said. That just made Dennis more determined. "I said to myself, 'I'm never going back to Dallas until I make the NBA,' " Dennis said. "I worked hard and kept it in my mind: 'I'm going to make something of myself. Start something and

finish it.' I didn't let the worst get the best of me."

Dennis entered Southeastern Oklahoma State in 1983. He didn't live in a dormitory. Instead, he lived with the Rich family on their farm in Bokchito, Oklahoma.

Dennis and Bryne Rich had met at a basketball camp in the summer of 1983. When Dennis and Bryne met, Bryne was very sad. He had been involved in a hunting accident in which a friend had been killed. Bryne had been depressed for a year. Dennis helped Bryne get over his sadness. And Bryne and the Riches welcomed Dennis into their family. They helped him adjust to life in Oklahoma. More important, the Riches helped Dennis settle down a bit. They helped him concentrate on school and basketball.

In three years at Southeastern Oklahoma, Dennis averaged 25.7 points and 15.7 rebounds per game. But because Southeastern Oklahoma is a small school, not many people knew how good he was. Before the 1986 draft, Dennis played went to some camps and played well against other top college players. The Detroit Pistons drafted him in the second round.

Dennis Rodman's College Statistics

		POINTS		ASSISTS	REBOUNDS
Season	**Games**	**Total**	**Average**	**Average**	**Average**
1983–84	30	779	26.0	0.8	13.1
1984–85	32	857	26.8	0.4	15.9
1985–86	34	829	24.4	0.8	17.8
Totals	**96**	**2,465**	**25.7**	**0.6**	**15.7**

Dennis didn't play a lot in his rookie season. But in his second season, 1987–88, he averaged 11.6 points and 8.6 rebounds per game. He also became known as one of the best defenders in the league. In 1989–90, he became a starter and won the NBA Defensive Player of the Year award.

Dennis won his second straight Defensive Player of the Year award in 1990–91. Then he decided to work on another part of his game: rebounding. In 1991–92, he led the league by averaging 18.7 rebounds per game. Dennis led the league in rebounding the next year as well.

Dennis's play was great. His behavior wasn't. In seven seasons with Detroit, he became almost as well known for the things he did off the court as for what he did on it. He skipped practices. Once, he even failed to show up for a road trip! The Pistons grew tired of Dennis's behavior. After the 1993 season, they traded him to the San Antonio Spurs for two players.

Dennis spent the 1993–94 and the 1994–95 seasons with the Spurs. He won two more rebounding titles and helped San Antonio become a great defensive team. But he continued to get into trouble. In both seasons, he was thrown out of more

AS THE WORM TURNS

As a kid, Dennis liked to play pinball. He wiggled his tall, skinny body so much when he played that he was given the nickname, the Worm. Dennis is still called Worm.

games and had more technical fouls than any other NBA player. In 1995, the Spurs decided they had had enough. Even though he had helped San Antonio to a league-leading 62–20 record, the Spurs traded Dennis to Chicago for Will Perdue, a backup center who hardly ever played.

Whenever the ball goes up, the chances are good that Dennis will come down with it.

NATHANIEL S. BUTLER/NBA PHOTOS

Dennis had led the league in rebounding four seasons in a row. He had made two All-Star teams and he had been named Defensive Player of the Year twice. But he also complained about teammates, criticized opponents, and whined about his contract. Some Bull players weren't sure that having Dennis on the team would be worth the aggravation.

Chicago coach Phil Jackson disagreed. He knew the Bulls really needed someone who could rebound. He

also thought he could convince Dennis to behave. Off the court, he could do whatever he wanted. But no matter what, Dennis had to behave on the court. Dennis agreed.

Dennis played great all season. He made the NBA's All-Defensive team for the sixth time and averaged 14.9 rebounds per game. It was the fifth straight time Dennis had led the league in rebounding. Only Moses Malone, who played for the Houston Rockets and the Philadelphia 76ers between 1980–81 and 1984–85, had led the league in rebounding five seasons in a row! Thanks to Dennis, the Bulls out-rebounded their opponents by 6.6 rebounds per game. The season before, they averaged only one more rebound per game than their opponents. On top of all that, Dennis had only one major run-in with league officials.

Dennis and the Bulls are a perfect fit. They need a rebounder, and Dennis loves to rebound. He doesn't care about scoring. Entering the 1996–97 season, he had averaged more than 10 points per game only once in his 10-season career.

"I rebound with a little flair, a little something extra," he says. "It's not for the crowd, it's just for me. Rebounding is how I express myself on the floor." The Bulls will be happy to have Dennis express himself for years to come.

Chapter Nine

Toni Kukoc

While the Bulls were winning three straight NBA titles from 1991 to 1993, it seemed the whole world was watching. In Europe, one man was paying particular attention to the Bulls' success. Toni Kukoc *[COO-coach]* was more than just a fan — he was the best basketball player in Europe. Toni was also Chicago's first-round draft pick in 1990. He had not yet joined the Bulls in 1990, but he looked forward to playing in the NBA some day.

"It was my dream to play with Michael Jordan," Toni said. "He was so amazing. I thought it would be an honor to be on the same court as him and get a chance to learn from him."

Toni Kukoc was born on September 18, 1968. He grew up in Split, Croatia, a small city on the Adriatic Sea. (When Toni was a boy, Croatia was part of Yugoslavia, a country in Eastern Europe near Austria and Italy. As a result of a war that began in 1991, Yugoslavia broke into several different countries, including Croatia.)

When Toni was young, his favorite sport was soccer. He didn't play basketball until he was about 15 years old.

Even then, if it hadn't been for luck, he might *never* have played. One day, Toni was running along a beach in his hometown when a local basketball coach noticed him. The coach thought Toni, who was already 6' 1" tall, might make a pretty good basketball player. Toni decided to give the sport a try. "At first, I didn't like basketball too much," Toni once said. "I liked soccer better."

Toni worked to improve his skills. He practiced before, during, and after school, every day. He learned all the fundamentals of passing and shooting. He was a *really* quick learner: He turned pro at age 17, a little more than two years after taking up the game! In his first four seasons, he was named European Player of the Year three times. With Toni leading the way, Croatia won the 1990 world championship and a silver medal at the 1992 Summer Olympics.

In 1992–93, his last pro season in Europe, Toni played for a team in Italy called Benetton Treviso. He averaged 19 points, 6.4 rebounds, and 5.2 assists per game. He had several quadruple doubles (meaning he had 10 or more

THE TEAM OF THE WORLD

There are only 25 players in the NBA who were born outside of the United States. The 1995–96 Chicago Bulls had four of them! The foreign-born Bulls in addition to Toni are Luc Longley (Australia), Bill Wennington (Canada) and Steve Kerr (Lebanon).

points in four different categories). Quadruple doubles are very rare! Fans began to call Toni the "Magic Johnson of Europe," because he played like the great Los Angeles Laker guard. Toni and Magic were as big and tall as a forward, but each of them had the skills of a point guard. Both players made passes that amazed fans and fooled opponents.

Name: **Toni Kukoc**
Birth Date: **September 18, 1968**
1st Season in NBA: **1993**
Height: **6' 11"**
Weight: **232 pounds**
Nickname: **Kuki**

U.S. basketball scouts noticed Toni's terrific play. In 1990, the Bulls drafted him. At the time, the political situation in Yugoslavia was very bad. Toni didn't want to leave his family because he was afraid something awful might happen. So he stayed in Europe. But by 1993, his parents had left Croatia and Toni had accomplished everything he could as a basketball player in Europe. It was time to come to America.

"My biggest reason is to prove to myself that I can play in the NBA," Toni said at the time. "The NBA is the best basketball in the world. I want the challenge. I'm ready."

The year before Toni joined the Bulls, he played for Croatia in the 1992 Summer Olympics. Scottie Pippen and Michael Jordan were on the U.S. Dream Team. They decided to show Toni what life in the NBA was like. They took it to Toni — hard. In an early game, they shut Toni down. He made just 2 of 11 shots and turned the ball over seven

times. But when Croatia played the U.S. again for the gold medal, Toni scored 16 points and had nine assists. Michael and Scottie were impressed. Afterward, Michael told Toni, "See you in the NBA."

Unfortunately, Toni wouldn't see Michael in the NBA for almost three years. Toni joined the Bulls in the summer of 1993, soon after the Bulls had won their third straight championship — and just before Michael retired. Toni was very disappointed. It looked like his dream of playing with Michael wouldn't come true.

Toni struggled through his first two NBA seasons. The competition was better than he had ever seen. He got burned a lot on defense — opponents would zoom past him and score easy baskets. Over time, though, Toni's defense improved. But Toni's passing and shooting skills were obvious from the start. In his first two seasons, his scoring average rose from 10.9 to 15.7 points per game. And when Michael returned to the NBA at the end of the 1995 season, Toni finally got his chance to play with his idol!

Michael liked playing with Toni. He really appreciated Toni's competitiveness. Like Michael, Toni *wants* to take

A MAN OF MANY NICKNAMES

When Toni played in Europe, he was known as Pink Panther, Alien, the Spider of Split, the Waiter, and Kuki. But when he was a kid, his nickname was "Feet." Toni didn't have fast feet. He had BIG feet!

the game-winning shot. When the pressure is on, great players want to be the hero. It was clear to Michael that Toni wanted to be great.

As much as Toni had been looking forward to playing with Michael, it wasn't easy at first. For one thing, Toni had been a starter in his first two NBA seasons. When Michael came back, Toni had to come off the bench. That was difficult for Toni, because he had always been a starter. Another problem was that Toni was star-struck. He was so amazed to be playing with Michael that he sometimes watched Michael and forgot to play his game!

As the 1995–96 season progressed, Toni became more and more comfortable coming off the bench. During a game against the Orlando Magic, Michael and Scottie Pippen were having bad nights. Toni took over. He made six 3-pointers and scored 24 points overall. "That was a turning point for this team," Michael said later. "Once Toni stopped watching me and started playing with me, we became a very dangerous team."

In 1995–96, Toni averaged 13.1 points per game and was Chicago's third-leading scorer. He also finished third on the team in assists (3.5), and third in minutes played (2,103). Thanks to his great play, Toni was named the NBA's Sixth Man of the Year, an award given to a player who isn't a starter (Toni started just 20 games in 1995–96). Toni had helped the Bulls become a very dangerous team. The Bulls helped Toni become one of the NBA's most dangerous players.

Chapter Ten

The Rest of the Best

Michael Jordan, Scottie Pippen, Dennis Rodman, and Toni Kukoc are great players. But even they would tell you that the Bulls couldn't have won an NBA title without a little help from their friends on the bench.

Many of the Bulls aren't very well known and don't receive much attention. But that doesn't mean they aren't valuable. Forward Jud Buechler played in 74 games. Guard Randy Brown played in 68. Neither player started even one game, but when they did play, Jud and Randy provided great defense and hit some important jump shots. Center Bill Wennington scored a little more than 5 points while playing just 15 minutes per game. Whenever Coach Phil Jackson needed a burst of offense or a bit of defense, Chicago's unsung heroes came through.

Here's a brief look at three other important Bulls.

LUC LONGLEY

Starting center Luc Longley will never be mistaken for an overpowering center like Los Angeles Laker Shaquille O'Neal. But as long as Luc plays for the Bulls, he doesn't *need* to be overpowering. He just needs to score a little, rebound a little, and play defense a lot.

SCOTT CUNNINGHAM/NBA PHOTOS

Off the court, Luc is laid back. But on the court, it's better to stay out of the big guy's way!

Luc does all of those things. In 1995–96, he averaged 9.1 points and 5.1 rebounds per game.

Luc is perfect for the Bulls. But when he first joined the NBA, he was a disappointment. He found out that what had worked well for him in college didn't work at all in the pros. The Minnesota Timberwolves had drafted Luc in the first round in 1991. But in 1994, after a little more than two

Name: **Luc Longley**
Birth Date: **January 19, 1969**
Height: **7' 2"**
Weight: **292 pounds**
1st Season in NBA: **1991**

seasons with the Wolves, Luc was traded to Chicago. "I had to completely revise my offensive game," he says. "I was just trying to shoot over people."

Luc is a laid-back, carefree guy. Sometimes it seems as if he isn't playing hard. His teammates and coaches get on him for that. During the 1995–96 playoffs, fans could see Michael Jordan yelling at Luc, "You're getting beat!" But that helped Luc focus. He scored 14 points in Game 1 of the Finals against the Seattle SuperSonics, and 19 points in Game 3.

Even if Luc had never won an NBA championship, he would still be famous — at least, in his own country! Luc is the first person from Australia to play in the NBA. Back home, the big game is Australian Rules Football, not basketball. But at 7' 2" and 292 pounds, Luc was born to play hoops!

RON HARPER

After Michael Jordan retired in October 1993, the Bulls knew they needed to find a new scoring threat. So, in 1994, they signed free agent Ron Harper.

For almost eight seasons, Ron had been one of the league's best and most exciting guards. Some people even compared him with Michael Jordan! Season in

and season out, Ron scored almost 20 points per game. But in his first season with Chicago, Ron had a difficult time adjusting to the Bulls' style of play. He scored only 6.9 points per game. In the playoffs, he hardly played at all. "I didn't know my basketball role," he says. "Half the time, I was horrible. It was embarrassing."

Ron turned things around in 1995–96. With Michael Jordan back in the lineup, Ron's role changed. Although he started almost every game, the Bulls didn't need him to score points. Chicago needed him to be a reliable shooter to take some pressure off Michael and Scottie Pippen. He was. Ron averaged just 7.4 points per game, but his shooting percentage was the highest it had been in five seasons. Even better for the Bulls, Ron was one of their best defenders all season.

Name: **Ron Harper**
Birth Date: **January 20, 1964**
Height: **6' 6"**
Weight: 216 pounds
1st Season in NBA: **1986**

"A lot of players don't accept their roles in this league," Ron told *The Chicago Tribune*. "And that's the key here. I know I play on a very good team and the main goal is to get that championship ring. It's not worrying about what you do as long as the team does well. I know my role. I didn't let my ego get in the way of the team."

ANDY HAYT/NBA PHOTOS

By pro basketball standards, Steve doesn't stand tall. But his shooting is huge!

STEVE KERR

In 1995–96, Steve Kerr played in every one of the Bulls' 82 games — and started in none of them! But that's okay with Steve, because that has been the story for most of his career.

In eight seasons, Steve has never averaged more than 8.6 points per game. He doesn't really rebound or block shots. He does make a few steals and dish out a few assists, but not many. What makes Steve so valuable is his deadly jump shot. In fact, Steve has made a higher percentage of his 3-point shots than anyone else in NBA history.

Steve's shooting ability is important for two reasons. First, it means he can score points in a hurry. Second, it forces other teams to guard him. When teams do that, they can't put two defenders on Michael Jordan or Scottie Pippen, so those two players have more room to move — and more chances to score.

Name: **Steve Kerr**
Birth Date: **September 27, 1965**
Height: **6' 3"**
Weight: **181 pounds**
1st Season in NBA: **1988**

Nothing has been easy for Steve. When he was in high school, only one college recruited him. The school wouldn't give him a scholarship. He was told he was too slow. The University of Arizona accepted him, but only to be a practice player.

During his freshman year, in 1984, Steve received the worst news of his life. His father, the president of American University in Beirut, Lebanon, had been murdered.

Through everything, Steve stayed strong. He continued to improve as a basketball player. In his sophomore year at Arizona, he became a starter. In 1988, he was selected by the Phoenix Suns in the second round of the NBA draft. Since then, Steve has bounced around a lot. He signed a free-agent contract with Chicago in 1993. The Bulls were his fourth team in six seasons. But none of that matters now. As long as Steve and his jump shot stay healthy, he has a home in Chicago.

Chapter Eleven

Statistics

1995–96 Regular-Season Statistics

Player	Games	POINTS Total	POINTS Average	ASSISTS Average	REBOUNDS Average
Michael Jordan	82	2,491	30.4	4.3	6.6
Scottie Pippen	77	1,496	19.4	5.9	6.4
Toni Kukoc	81	1,065	13.1	3.5	3.9
Luc Longley	62	564	9.1	1.9	5.1
Steve Kerr	82	688	8.4	2.3	1.3
Ron Harper	80	594	7.4	2.6	2.7
Dennis Rodman	64	351	5.5	2.5	14.9
Bill Wennington	71	376	5.3	0.7	2.5
Jack Haley	1	5	5.0	0.0	2.0
John Salley	17	36	2.1	0.9	2.5
Jud Buechler	74	278	3.8	0.8	1.5
Dickey Simpkins	60	216	3.6	0.6	2.6
James Edwards	28	98	3.5	0.4	1.4
Jason Caffey	57	182	3.2	0.4	1.9
Randy Brown	68	185	2.7	1.0	1.0

1995–96 Award Winners

- **Michael Jordan**: MVP, regular season and playoffs; first team All-NBA
- **Toni Kukoc**: NBA Sixth Man of the Year (awarded to the best player in the league who doesn't start a majority of his team's games)
- **Scottie Pippen**: First team All-NBA
- **Phil Jackson (head coach)**: NBA Coach of the Year
- **Jerry Krause (general manager)**: NBA Executive of the Year

The Road to the 1995–96 Championship

FIRST ROUND
Chicago Bulls 3, Miami Heat 0

Chicago 102, Miami 85
Chicago 106, Miami 75
Chicago 112, Miami 91

EASTERN CONFERENCE SEMI-FINALS
Chicago Bulls 4, New York Knicks 1

Chicago 91, New York 84
Chicago 91, New York 80
New York 102, Chicago 99
Chicago 94, New York 91
Chicago 94, New York 81

EASTERN CONFERENCE FINALS
Chicago Bulls 4, Orlando Magic 0

Chicago 121, Orlando 83
Chicago 93, Orlando 88
Chicago 86, Orlando 67
Chicago 106, Orlando 101

NBA FINALS
Chicago Bulls 4, Seattle SuperSonics 2

Chicago 107, Seattle 90
Chicago 92, Seattle 88
Chicago 108, Seattle 86
Seattle 107, Chicago 86
Seattle 89, Chicago 78
Chicago 87, Seattle 75

The First Three Championships

1991 NBA FINALS
Chicago Bulls 4, Los Angeles Lakers 1

Los Angeles 93, Chicago 91
Chicago 107, Los Angeles 86
Chicago 104, Los Angeles 96 (overtime)
Chicago 97, Los Angeles 82
Chicago 108, Los Angeles 101

1992 NBA FINALS
Chicago Bulls 4, Portland Trail Blazers 2

Chicago 122, Portland 89
Portland 115, Chicago 104 (overtime)
Chicago 94, Portland 84
Portland 93, Chicago 88
Chicago 119, Portland 106
Chicago 97, Portland 93

1993 NBA FINALS
Chicago Bulls 4, Phoenix Suns 2

Chicago 100, Phoenix 92
Chicago 111, Phoenix 108
Phoenix 129, Chicago 121 (triple overtime)
Chicago 111, Phoenix 105
Phoenix 108, Chicago 98
Chicago 99, Phoenix 98